Walki... ...Wild, Weird and
Wack...
Karen
AR B.L.: 2.5
Points: 0.5

S0-AAK-505

Walking is

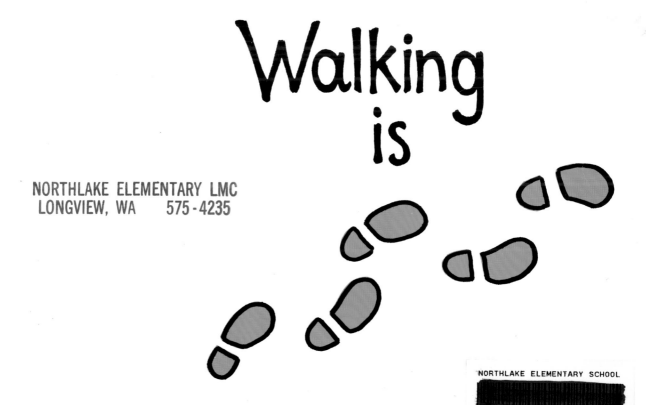

Walking is

Wild Weird and Wacky

written and illustrated by
Karen Kerber

LANDMARK EDITIONS, INC.

P.O. Box 4469 • 1402 Kansas Avenue • Kansas City, Missouri 64127
(816) 241-4919

Revised Edition

Second Printing

COPYRIGHT © 1981, 1985, 1989 BY KAREN KERBER

International Standard Book Number: 0-933849-29-X (LIB.BDG.)

Library of Congress Cataloging-in-Publication Data
Kerber, Karen, 1969-   Rev. ed.
    p.   cm.
    Walking is wild, weird and wacky.
    Summary: Describes a variety of ways of walking, such as strolling like a
sardine, twirling like a tornado, and pouncing like a pogo stick.

    1. Children's writings.
    [1. Walking—Fiction.   2. Motion—Fiction.
    3. Children's writings.]

I. Title
PZ7.K453Wal   1989   [E]—dc20   89-13547

Editorial Coordinator: Nancy R. Thatch
Creative Coordinator: David Melton

Printed in the United States of America

Landmark Editions, Inc.
P.O. Box 4469
1402 Kansas Avenue
Kansas City, Missouri 64127
(816) 241-4919

WALKING IS WILD, WEIRD AND WACKY

At twelve years of age, Karen Kerber was enrolled in a Written & Illustrated by... Workshop that I conducted at The Lindenwood Colleges in St. Charles, Missouri.

"Karen has *school burnout,*" her mother told me, "and she needs the creative challenge your workshop offers."

But Karen was reluctant to attend the workshop. She told me she would write a book, but she didn't want to illustrate one because, she said, "I can't draw a straight line."

"Then make all the lines wiggly and waggly," I quickly replied. And that's exactly what Karen did, in the hope that I would not like her drawings and she would not have to finish the course.

The opposite happened. I loved her drawings! The composition of the colorful illustrations, as well as the sly humor and playful alliteration of her narrative, bedazzled me. They still do.

At first glance, one might think that Karen's illustrations are a child's drawings. But upon more careful observation, the viewer should begin to realize that Karen's illustrations are no more children's drawings than are those done by Picasso, Chagall, or Miró.

Her illustrations are indeed sophisticated, and they cleverly display exceptional skill and imagination. In the flow of line and color, Karen satirizes human forms and projects them into the personalities of nonhuman animals. The worm is almost a worm, but it isn't really a worm. It is wearing trousers and possesses other human qualities. The snail is almost a snail, but not quite. But the personality of a snail is developed through free-flowing shapes of color, wrapped in a continuation of circular black lines. Even the rock has a stylized personality of its very own.

Karen playfully teases our eyes with an abundance of visual surprises. The more one looks, the more one sees. I have seen her illustrations more than 5,000 times for I have shown them in slides to students and teachers throughout the nation. Every time I look at them, I am delighted because I see something new and exciting in each projected image.

When Landmark Editions decided to publish books by students, there was no doubt about which book we should publish first — WALKING IS WILD, WEIRD AND WACKY. But because Karen's original workshop book was three years old and had gathered finger prints and smudges, we brought her to our offices to redo all the illustrations. At that time I insisted that she duplicate all of the illustrations without altering or improving them in any way. It was a terrible thing for me to do because no self-respecting adult author/illustrator should have to put up with such nonsense, and children shouldn't either. Now I know better, and I encourage all of our student author/illustrators to improve their work for publication.

Now, at last, Karen has been given the opportunity to make such improvements in WALKING. In order for us to place her book in a heavy-duty, reinforced library binding, we had to add eight pages. So at twenty years of age, Karen was asked if she would set her mind back in time and creatively become a twelve-year-old again to prepare the necessary additions and changes. This was by no means an easy task for her. But Karen met the challenge head-on, and we at Landmark had a wonderful time seeing the new images take form.

It is with great pleasure that Landmark introduces the revised edition of Karen's extraordinary book for you to read, observe and enjoy.

— David Melton
Creative Coordinator
Landmark Editions, Inc.

Prancing like a Pony is Peculiar.

Rambling like a Rock
is hazardous
to your health.

Sauntering like a Snail
is
S...l...u...g...g...i...s...h.

Treading
like a Turtle
is
tiring.

Waltzing like a Walrus is Wobbly.

Traveling like a
Telephone Pole
Elevates your Elbows
(and gets you nowhere!)

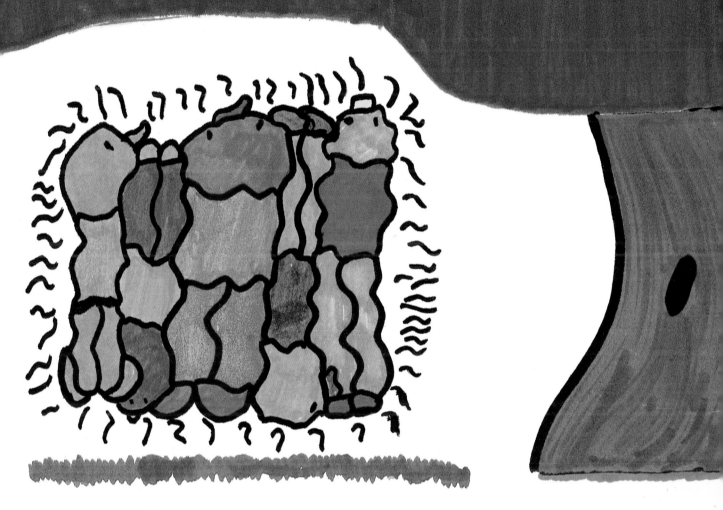

Strolling like a Sardine
is CRAMPED and Smelly.

Twirling like a Tornado is Terrifying!

Slithering like a Snake is Sensational.

Parading like a
Peacock is Proud.

Ambling like an Armadillo is Amusing.

Whirling like a Windmill is
Wild, Weird and
Wacky.
But...

...Marching like Me is

MARVE

BOOKS FOR STUDENTS

— WINNERS OF THE NATIONAL WRITTEN

by Aruna Chandrasekhar, age 9
Houston, Texas

A touching and timely story! When the lives of many otters are threatened by a huge oil spill, a group of concerned people come to their rescue. Wonderful illustrations.
Printed Full Color
ISBN 0-933849-33-8

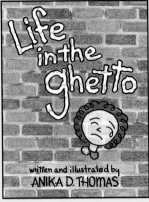

by Anika D. Thomas, age 13
Pittsburgh, Pennsylvania

A compelling autobiography! A young girl's heartrending account of growing up in a tough, inner-city neighborhood. The illustrations match the mood of this gripping story.
Printed Two Colors
ISBN 0-933849-34-6

by Cara Reichel, age 15
Rome, Georgia

Elegant and eloquent! A young stonecutter vows to create a great statue for his impoverished village. But his fame almost stops him from fulfilling that promise.
Printed Two Colors
ISBN 0-933849-35-4

by Jonathan Kahn, age 9
Richmond Heights, Ohio

A fascinating nature story! Patulous, a prairie rattle searches for food, he mus avoid the claws and fangs of enemies.
Printed Full Color
ISBN 0-933849-36-2

by Adam Moore, age 9
Broken Arrow, Oklahoma

A remarkable true story! When Adam was eight years old, he fell and ran an arrow into his head. With rare insight and humor, he tells of his ordeal and his amazing recovery.
Printed Two Colors
ISBN 0-933849-24-9

by Michael Aushenker, age 19
Ithaca, New York

Chomp! Chomp! When Arthur forgets to feed his goat, the animal eats everything in sight. A very funny story — good to the last bite. The illustrations are terrific.
Printed Full Color
ISBN 0-933849-28-1

by Leslie Ann MacKeen, age 9
Winston-Salem, North Carolina

Loaded with fun and puns! When Jeremiah T. Fitz's car stops running, several animals offer suggestions for fixing it. The results are hilarious. The illustrations are charming.
Printed Full Color
ISBN 0-933849-19-2

by Elizabeth Haidle, age 13
Beaverton, Oregon

A very touching story! The iest Elfkin learns to che friendship of others after an injured snail and befri orphaned boy. Absolutely b
Printed Full Color
ISBN 0-933849-20-6

by Amy Hagstrom, age 9
Portola, California

An exciting western! When a boy and an old Indian try to save a herd of wild ponies, they discover a lost canyon and see the mystical vision of the Great White Stallion.
Printed Full Color
ISBN 0-933849-15-X · Library Binding

by Isaac Whitlatch, age 11
Casper, Wyoming

The true confessions of a devout vegetable hater! Isaac tells ways to avoid and dispose of the "slimy green things." His colorful illustrations provide a salad of laughter and mirth.
Printed Full Color
ISBN 0-933849-16-8

by Dav Pilkey, age 19
Cleveland, Ohio

A thought-provoking parable! Two kings halt an arms race and learn to live in peace. This outstanding book launched Dav's career. He now has seven more books published.
Printed Full Color
ISBN 0-933849-22-2

by Karen Kerber, age 12
St. Louis, Missouri

A delightfully playful book is loaded with clever allitera gentle humor. Karen's bri ored illustrations are com wiggly and waggly strokes
Printed Full Color
ISBN 0-933849-29-X

To obtain Contest Rules, send a self-addressed, business-size envelope, stamped with .58 postag

...OO MUCH ...CK OR TREAT

WRITTEN AND ILLUSTRATED BY ...AYNA MILLER

...Miller, age 19
...ville, Ohio

...iest Halloween ever! When ... the Rabbit takes all the ...is friends get even. Their ...scheme includes a haunted ...nd mounds of chocolate.
...ll Color
...3849-37-0

Problems at the North Pole

written & illustrated by Lauren Peters

by Lauren Peters, age 7
Kansas City, Missouri

The Christmas that almost wasn't! When Santa Claus takes a vacation, Mrs. Claus and the elves go on strike. Toys aren't made. Cookies aren't baked. Super illustrations.
Printed Full Color
ISBN 0-933849-25-7

the Legend of SIR MIGUEL

written and illustrated by MICHAEL CAIN

by Michael Cain, age 11
Annapolis, Maryland

A glorious tale of adventure! To become a knight, a young man must face a beast in the forest, a spell-binding witch, and a giant bird that guards a magic oval crystal.
Printed Full Color
ISBN 0-933849-26-5

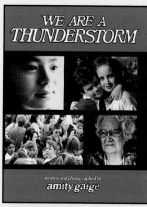

WE ARE A THUNDERSTORM

written and photographed by amity gaige

by Amity Gaige, age 16
Reading, Pennsylvania

A lyrical blend of poetry and pho-tographs! Amity's sensitive poems offer thought-provoking ideas and amusing insights. This lovely book is one to be savored and enjoyed.
Printed Full Color
ISBN 0-933849-27-3

...dy McFinley and the ...at Grey Grimly

...Heidi Salter

...Salter, age 19
...ey, California

...nd wonderful! To save her ...gination, a young girl must ... the Great Grey Grimly ...The narrative is filled with ... Vibrant illustrations.
...ll Color
...849-21-4

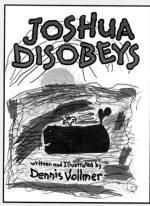

JOSHUA DISOBEYS

Written and Illustrated by Dennis Vollmer

by Dennis Vollmer, age 6
Grove, Oklahoma

A baby whale's curiosity gets him into a lot of trouble. GUINNESS BOOK OF RECORDS lists Dennis as the youngest author/illustrator of a published book.
Printed Full Color
ISBN 0-933849-12-5

THE HALF & HALF DOG

written and illustrated by LISA GROSS

by Lisa Gross, age 12
Santa Fe, New Mexico

A touching story of self-esteem! A puppy is laughed at because of his unusual appearance. His search for acceptance is told with sensitivity and humor. Wonderful illustrations.
Printed Full Color
ISBN 0-933849-13-3

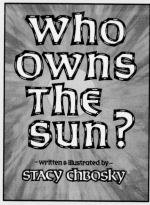

WHO OWNS THE SUN?

– written & illustrated by – STACY CHBOSKY

by Stacy Chbosky, age 14
Pittsburgh, Pennsylvania

A powerful plea for freedom! This emotion-packed story of a young slave touches an essential part of the human spirit. Made into a film by Disney Educational Productions.
Printed Full Color
ISBN 0-933849-14-1

THE ...RAGON OF ...ORD

...written and illustrated by ...AVID McADOO

...McAdoo, age 14
...eld, Missouri

...ng intergalactic adventure! ...stant future, a courageous ...efends a kingdom from a ...om outer space. Astound-...illustrations.
...otone
...849-23-0

PUNT, PASS & POINT!

written & illustrated by BONNIE-ALISE LEGGAT

by Bonnie-Alise Leggat, age 8
Culpeper, Virginia

Amy J. Kendrick wants to play foot-ball, but her mother wants her to become a ballerina. Their clash of wills creates hilarious situations. Clever, delightful illustrations!
Printed Full Color
ISBN 0-933849-39-7

NINA'S MAGIC

written and illustrated by Lisa Kirsten Butenhoff

by Lisa Kirsten Butenhoff, age 13
Woodbury, Minnesota

The people of a Russian village face the winter without warm clothes or enough food. Then their lives are improved by a young girl's gifts. A tender story with lovely illustrations.
Printed Full Color
ISBN 0-933849-40-0

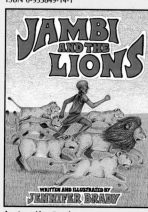

JAMBI AND THE LIONS

WRITTEN AND ILLUSTRATED BY JENNIFER BRADY

by Jennifer Brady, age 17
Columbia, Missouri

When poachers capture a pride of lions, a native boy tries to free the animals. A skillfully told story. Glowing illustrations illuminate this African adventure.
Printed Full Color
ISBN 0-933849-41-9

...EST FOR STUDENTS, Landmark Editions, Inc., P.O. Box 4469, Kansas City, MO 64127.

Jayna Miller
age 19

Lauren Peters
age 7

Michael Cain
age 11

Heidi Salter
age 19

Amity Gaige
age 16

Dennis Vollmer
age 6

Lisa Gross
age 12

Stacy Chbosky
age 14

Karen Kerber
age 12

David McAdoo
age 14

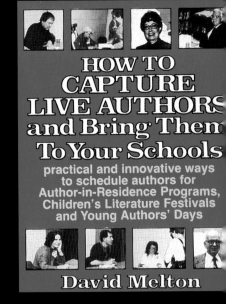